The Power of Writing:
A Guide to Journaling

A Self-Study
by L.A. Ridley

ISBN: 979-8-89589-876-5

Overview

The Power of Writing is a 9-week self-study designed to help aspiring writers engage in and embrace writing as a lifestyle. Whether you are wanting to find a creative outlet, use writing to process, record your thoughts, start a diary, embark on writing a short story, screenplay, or novel, or simply want to make writing a habit, this self-study provides tips and prompts that you can use to do so.

Author L.A. Ridley holds a doctoral degree in English and teaches composition, literature, and communication at the university level.

The Power of Writing

Lesson Outline

Guidelines for this Writing Course

1. The goal of this study is self discovery and reflection. It is not designed to tell you how to solve all of life's problems or reveal some grand advice from renowned experts. Rather, no one is an expert on your own life except you. You are the master. As William Ernest Henley writes in "Invictus": "I am the master of my fate: I am the captain of my soul." Make this your mantra as you move through this course, as it is designed to be a journey in which you are indeed the captain—of both your fate and your soul. There is no greater truth in your life than this. No one can guide your life's ship any better than you can. Hopefully, this self-study can chart new waters for you.

2. This class is not a race. It is designed for one lesson per week, but you can set your own pace. However, the more time you reflect on each lesson, the more meaningful it will be. The hope is that you read the lesson and then spend the week writing and reflecting on it. The questions are designed to serve as springboards for your reflections, but you are encouraged to write beyond the scope of what they address.

3. Attempt every question; however, if a question causes pain or emotion that you are not prepared to face, skip it. You can always come back to it later (or not at all).

4. Be as honest with yourself as you can in your responses.

5. Keep in mind that even if you take every step to ensure your writing will be private, there may come a time when someone, even without your permission, will read it. Do not write anything that might lead to consequences you are not prepared to face. If you write about your intentions to harm someone or yourself and someone reads that, there will be an intervention. While you are encouraged to be transparent, you need to be careful with how much you share.

6. Do not worry about writing conventions in your responses. This is not a grammar or composition class.

7. Keep in mind that writing is dependent on your current state of mind. Feelings and emotions are variable and change from day to day, sometimes even hour to hour, depending on your circumstances. What you write one day may not reflect how you feel the next.

8. The key to journaling is grace and space. Give yourself both.

9. Writing is one aspect of your life that cannot be controlled by anyone. As long as you have a pen and paper, you can write anywhere, any time, any place. You have complete control over what you write; however, remember there are always consequences to every action, even writing.

10. Do not put pressure on yourself to write or complete a lesson. If you aren't feeling it on a certain day, then don't force it. Take a break and come back to it when you are in a better place mentally and emotionally.

Introduction to the Power of Writing

With so much going on in our world today, the electronic word has become a very powerful tool. Think about all the times in recent days that you have been brought to anger, to sadness, to joy, to despair, and so many other deeply felt emotions just by something that you have read—likely on your phone or computer.

Technology is creating situations that would have been impossible just twenty years ago—some good and some bad—for a whole new world. We can have face-to-face video conferences with someone on the other side of the globe, but on the same day, sit in a quiet room with our family members, while everyone has their head buried in a smartphone, without a word being uttered.

Every era has had its ups and downs and its share of grief, struggles, and heartaches, and this one has a whole new set of trials and tribulations. While we all have our own ways of coping with the trials that cause us to stagger and fall, one approach that our ancestors discovered—one that charted and documented so much of history—was writing it down.

If the scribes of previous centuries changed the world through their writing, then why can't we also see it for what it is: a powerful tool that can shape and mold our lives, or at the least, record our journeys during this time on the earth? Through the written word, we can record history, process what is happening in our lives, praise and thank our deity if we are people of faith, chart our mental and emotional paths, set goals for our life in general, and inspire others who may be experiencing some of the same joys and pains we are.

In short, writing has the power to change our own lives, as well as the lives of others, if only we could learn how to use it. There are several concepts to keep in mind as we begin this journey:

- We do not have to be good writers or know proper grammar to be effective writers for our writing to be impactful; however, we can prevent miscommunication if we know how to write.
- We do not need to share our writing for it to serve a purpose or initiate change.
- In our writing, we do not need to be politically correct or give canned or expected responses; rather, it is more effective when we speak from our hearts and be honest with ourselves.

- Journaling is not social media where we have to fake it or portray an image. It's about being real.
- We need to be consistent and deliberate with our writing if it is to make a difference in our lives. Like anything else, such as exercising or eating well, it requires commitment and discipline.

The Benefits of Writing

When one looks up the definition of the verb, *write*, many alternate verbs are used: communicate, form words, express, execute, compose, among others. All of these verbs involve the act of sitting down with pen and paper or at a computer and putting into print or recording what we are thinking in our minds. While a simple process externally, it is quite a complicated process internally: one that can be easily completed by some, but can be a monstrous struggle for others.

Purposes of Writing

Before we begin any writing venture, whether a journal, email, letter, social media post, poem, short story, application for a job, or even on a grand scale, a novel, we must first consider both our purpose and our audience for writing. Generally speaking, there are various purposes for writing. In general, when we write something that is to be shared with others, we write to inform, we write to persuade, we write to entertain, and we write to inspire. Another one that permeates our current society is that we write to incite negativity or anger—something we have seen more of recently than in years past.

If, on the other hand, we are writing just for ourselves, writing can take on other purposes: we can write to process, we can write to cope, and we can write to record—our pasts, our presents, and our aspirations for the future. When we are writing for ourselves, we are writing to sort through what is happening in our lives, to make sense of life, to communicate with our deity, and to deal with the pain or joy we may be experiencing. In doing so, the act becomes very much an internal act, in addition to being an external act. While the other purposes call for external audiences: teachers, classmates, friends, family members, editors, fans, potential employers, blog readers, social media followers, etc., when we are writing to process, we are writing for an audience of one: me.

Writing to process has been known to be therapeutic for the mind and soul and have significant effects on the body. Study after study shows how depression and grief can be combated and even overcome by people sharing and processing their stories.

Laurie Nadel, a psychotherapist and journalist who covered many of the world's political hot spots, eased her stress by journaling: "I thought that if I could write everything down, I could stay safe," Nadel said in an interview. Now, she has a book on the subject and encourages her clients to journal as a means of therapy.

James Pennebaker, a distinguished professor at the University of Texas, used journaling as a way to combat his failing marriage, which was causing him to drink, smoke, and become depressed. He started writing freely about his marriage and other struggles in his life. As he wrote, his depression lifted; he began to fix his marriage and see other possibilities in his life.

Pennebaker's experience sparked forty years of research about the links between writing and emotional processing. His studies involved dividing people into groups and asking them to write about their life experiences. Many ended up sharing stories about sexual abuse, failure, loss, illness, and death. Through these studies, Pennebaker found that the people who wrote about emotionally charged episodes experienced improvement in their physical and mental well-being. In the months after the writing sessions, they had lower blood pressure, improved immune function, and fewer visits to the doctor. These are just two examples of professionals who used writing in their own lives to process what they were going through, only to lead to breakthroughs in the lives of others.

Even though they did not set out to write for an audience, eventually that is what happened, and their readers became active contributors to their own journeys. As we consider our own audience, there is something we need to think about: there may come a time when the purpose of our writing may shift, and as such, our audience will change as well. Even though we are initially writing only for self, our audience may at some point expand beyond that. For example, we may decide, either on our own or through the prompting of others, to share a journal or testimony on a blog, with a friend, or with a wider audience in a public gathering. If we are writing for one of the other purposes that involve an external audience, it is crucial that we consider who that audience is and what their belief systems may be before we share.

We must keep in mind that even though our writing may be therapeutic or helpful to us, it may not be so for other people. On the other hand, it may be life changing. We have to be, like other times in life, cognizant of the journeys of others. As we begin our own journey, it is important to think about this.

Writing Can Be Immortal

Another thought about writing that makes it appealing to many people: there is a chance that what we write will outlive us. There is truly something immortal about penning our thoughts and emotions into tangible, written form. It is interesting to see my own writings from years past, to go back and read what I have written, and wonder what people will think of them when I am gone if they happen to come across them.

Even on an informal, personal level, I have found letters written from my father to my mother, recipes from my grandmother, prayers my mother wrote down years ago, and many other artifacts from my parents' estate that contain thoughts and emotions expressed by them written years before. I will hopefully pass these along to my own children, and one can only guess where they will end up. So, as we begin this journey, think about where your own writings may find their way.

My goal for this study is that you find some value and purpose in writing and that you see how powerful it can be, both for you personally and for others as well. Even if you never plan to share a word that you write, if nothing else, it can help you dialogue with yourself and learn a few things along the way. Sometimes getting all of the thoughts, feelings, and emotions that are churning in your head out and into some tangible form can be healing and enlightening. My hope is that you develop a consistent habit of writing and make it a lifestyle in the coming weeks ahead. I also hope you can begin and complete those long-buried writing projects that perhaps might even be a bucket-list item or long-sought-after dream. Whatever the case, I hope you come out of this with a new appreciation for the power of writing, and what it can mean for both you and others. There is much to be taught and learned through the power of writing.

Writing for Reflection

1. Describe your past experiences with journaling.

2. Does the idea of keeping a journal sound appealing? Why/why not?

3. How as the written word changed our world, in your opinion?

4. Discuss how writing can be both external and internal.

5. What is your primary purpose for writing?

6. Why do you think writing has therapeutic properties?

7. Have you ever used writing as a coping mechanism in your life? Explain.

8. What would be the advantages of journaling in your own life?

The Path to Consistent Writing

Do you remember as a child recording an experience or sharing a memory in writing that has resurfaced in your time as an adult? Did you keep a diary as a child? Did you ever have the privilege or opportunity to read a diary written by someone you love? If so, then you have had some experiences with the kind of writing that is known as journaling.

Journaling can have many faces and come in many forms. Essentially, a journal is a person's record of events, thoughts, or feelings; it can be shared with the public (i.e. in a blog or post), or it can be deeply private and kept under lock and key under your bed. It can be handwritten in a book made specifically for that purpose, or it can be typed and written in electronic form that can later be edited and revised. Journaling is probably the most intense and personal type of writing that exists and can serve many purposes in a person's life.

Importance of Journaling

Why is journaling important? Why do writers keep journals? The reasons are as varied as the people who write them. There are many advantages to keeping a journal and recording your thoughts and emotions.

1. A journal can be used as a historical account to serve for future generations. Many times journals can be passed down from one family member to another and can record important life moments and dates, for example, marriages, family gatherings, deaths, vacations, and other important events that could be lost if not recorded.
2. A journal can be a log or record of personal events that will help preserve such memories for a lifetime. Journals can help writers keep track of their own lives and can be used as reference months or even years after events and feelings are recorded. It is nice to be able to go back and read what you were thinking at various stages in your life and see when events occurred and what they meant to you at the time.
3. A journal can help a writer process thoughts, feelings, and events as a means of finding acceptance or closure. It can also simply serve a means for venting or sharing so that such feelings do not remain bottled inside. Studies have shown that people who write down what they are feeling feel less stress, as journaling is a means of coping and sorting through struggles and obstacles. Some writers even report being able to let grudges and other negative feelings go after they have recorded them on paper or on the computer. We all have heard of the notion of writing a letter to a person or about a hurtful situation but then tearing it up and throwing it away in lieu of sending it. Doing so can help us work through thoughts or feelings we have and in some cases get to the sources of why we are feeling such emotions.

4. A journal can be a means of fighting depression and coping with grief and loss. Many therapists encourage, and some even require that their patients who suffer from depression or grief keep a journal while undergoing therapy. Research has proven this to be beneficial in battling these negative experiences and emotions. Some doctors even claim patients are able to be weaned from antidepressants after using journaling as a way to cope with depression. While it may not be a cure all for these ailments, it certainly has proven to be an important part of battling mental illness.

When it comes to journaling, there are a number of approaches a writer can take, and there are various types of journals that you can keep. Before you begin journaling, you will need to consider two important factors that every writer should take into account before beginning any writing endeavor: a) what is your purpose in writing? and b) who is your audience?

Let's think about the following questions as we begin this journey.
- Why do you want to keep a journal?
- Do you want or hope to allow anyone else to read your journal?
- Would you be upset if someone did?
- If your wish is for your journal to remain private, do you have a secure location where that can be granted?
- What do you hope to gain by keeping a journal?
- Do you want to handwrite your thoughts or type them on a computer? Again, if security is an issue, how will you plan to keep any electronic trail private?
- Do you ever hope to share or publish your journal, even if your goal right now is to keep it private?
- Will you have the time to be consistent in writing in your journal? If so, how often do you plan on writing?
- In short, who is your intended audience for your journal, both in the present and future?
- If you were to become ill, incapacitated, or worse, what would the ramifications be if someone were to read your journal?

Tips for Keeping a Journal

While there are most definitely no set rules when it comes to journaling, the following are a few suggestions or tips that will make the process all that you hope it can be.

1. Date your entries. While this may be common sense, many people forget this all-important piece of information. Without the dates, you have no idea when your entries were written, which is vital years later when the journal is revisited. Remember to make sure you record the year as well.
2. Keep it in a place where it is safe from others if you are uncomfortable with people reading it. It can be a painful experience when someone either mistakenly or intentionally reads your thoughts when you were not desiring for that to occur. The inherent danger in journaling comes into play here, since journals truly are some of

the most private pieces of writing that exist. It is a gateway into your mind and allows people close to you to read your most intimate thoughts. If you are fearful of this occurring, you need to be sure to take the steps necessary to protect your journal: lock it in a safe place with a key or put a passcode on an electronic journal.

3. Be honest and transparent. There is no point in keeping a journal if it does not reveal complete honesty. Again, do not create a work that serves other people; this is the one piece of writing in your entire life that has no agenda except your own. Be true to that agenda and to yourself.

4. Be consistent and write faithfully. No journal is going to be effective unless you write often. If you write journal entries only once a year, you will not be able to see change or growth, or follow the thought processes that emerge with maturity, experience, and day-to-day living. It is important to make journaling a habit and part of your routine, either daily or weekly. Write at the same time each day or the same day each week to provide your best opportunities for success. Procrastination and busyness are two obstacles that prevent most writers—not just journal writers—from writing, and consistency is the best way to combat those.

5. Follow a common theme or style. The best way to prevent writer's block and to keep yourself writing is to stay on track with one single approach or theme at a time. If you want to change it up later, you can create multiple journals or go back and forth. However, staying focused and consistent on one theme at a time will prevent you from jumping around, losing interest, and forgoing the project altogether when disorganization sets in. Writer's block can also be avoided if you stay true to one theme as it provides a framework on which you can build as you write.

6. Do not concern yourself with grammar, mechanics, or spelling. This is the one time in your writing endeavors that you need not worry about the structure of your writing. Who cares if you have spelling errors or commas in the wrong place? If you decide to publish your journal later, it will likely go through an intense editing process, which will alleviate any errors you might make along the way. Focusing on these matters and/or concerning yourself with them while you are writing can take up valuable time and divert your focus off the content of your material.

7. Write only when you feel inclined and the need to share. A journal entry should never be forced. Even though it is important to be consistent, again, the journal is the one piece of writing in your life that does not have an agenda, deadline, or limitations. It will not follow a formula or have to adhere to any standards other than what you impose. As such, make it your own and write when you want, how you want, and what you want. You will never regret having a journal as long as you are true to yourself and to your thoughts.

8. Be sure to have a plan of what will happen in the event that you become ill, incapacitated, or—there's no easy way to say this—die! If you keep a journal for a lifetime, it is one of those inevitable realities we have to face. At some point, someone other than you will find it and read your thoughts. Even though you will likely be too ill to care or long departed from this world, your journal will serve as part of your legacy, and you need to make sure the legacy you are leaving behind is one that you want to share. Be aware of the fact that your loved ones may read your journal, and if doing so may cause them pain, you need to figure out another plan for your journal after you pass

on. Even though it is important to be honest in your writings, it is also important to be aware that words are the most powerful weapons on this earth. They can and do destroy, even if we are gone. If you don't want someone to be hurt by your words, then it is best that you dispose of those writings that you are using for therapeutic purposes. Keep the benign and positive events and experiences for your loved ones to read. You can also make sure your will states a plan for the disposal of your journal as you would for other important and valuable items that you own. Be aware that your journal will likely outlive you, and be cognizant of the legacy you are leaving behind in the words and pages of this valuable work.

As you can see, creating a journal can provide a wonderful experience for both you and other people in your life. If you decide to begin this journey, remember to always be true to yourself and follow your own beat. In the next part of this lesson, we will discuss the different types of journals.

Types of Journal Projects

The type of writing project or journal you decide to write will depend on a number of factors. First off, you need to decide how often you can write and how long you will be able to write during each writing session. This will determine both your approach and the type of journal you decide to write.

There are various approaches to journaling. Some are more private than others. Some are more event-based, while others are more feeling and thought-centered. The important concept to remember is that it is best to keep some kind of consistency or theme if you want to prevent writer's block and continue the momentum of your project. If you sit down every day to write but have no agenda, it may not always be easy to come up with topics to write about, especially on hard or stressful days. Your mood will always affect not just what you write, but how you write and why you write. Having some kind of agenda or theme will help keep you on track and motivated to write. You can always write one type of journal for a designated time, for example, six months or a year, and then switch to another journal after you tire of a certain approach or are ready to try something new.

Following are some suggestions for your journal:

1. **Begin a diary of your life story.** You can start in the present, or you can write about your childhood and/or growing up years. Or you can start in the past and work your way to the present by recording events chronologically. Be sure to give dates and important details that you can remember. You may need to research some facts if you cannot recall them. If your purpose is to record an honest recollection of your life, do not embellish or make up facts that you cannot remember. If there is no way of finding out the questionable information, then record what you do know and omit the rest of it. You can organize these events chronologically and write them in that order, or write about the events that are clear in your mind and organize your thoughts later.

2. **Write a topic-related journal.** These journals often find themselves in a public forum, such as a blog, and are meant to focus heavily on a topic or certain content. An example of this would be a recipe or health blog. These are meant to target your own journey in a certain area of your life and can be helpful when focusing specifically on one content area, rather than a more diverse series of topics.

3. **Write a memory journal and recall times in your life that have special meaning.** This type of journal is not designed to be a chronological recap of your life, but rather a series of certain memories that you can recall. It can be organized either topically or chronologically. Potential topics could be: holidays, vacations, birthdays, births, deaths, important people (friends, family, etc.), family memories, academic endeavors, social occasions, regrets, spiritual experiences, childhood hangouts or toys, school memories, world events, tragedies, sources or times of growth, or painful lessons. This type of journal is focused on groups or segments of memories, not a recap of your life.

4. **Write a short story or novel that you hope to publish one day.** You can journal your creative thoughts into fiction and begin writing a short story or novel. Such can be modeled after true events, for example, traumatic events that you can fictionalize to prevent revelation of truth. Or you can create a world and characters all your own that you may hope to publish one day. Writing a novel is on the bucket list of so many people, and it might be on yours as well. If such a venture starts out under the guise of a journal, it may help with the flow of thoughts and remove the pressure of undertaking the daunting task of writing your first novel.

5. **Write a series of poems or songs.** If you are more of a lyrical writer, you may choose to make your journal a grouping of these creative works. They can be reflections of your thoughts and might even outline certain events in your life, like many songs or poems do, although these tend to be more eloquently written than prose. You can choose to write stanzas in separate writing sessions, or write a longer song or poem as inspiration hits. Song lyrics and poems can touch people in ways that other creative works may not necessarily be able to do. If that kind of inspiration is calling, it is best not to avoid it.

6. **Once a day or even once a week, choose a piece of writing that you come across in your life and respond to it.** This can be a media report, Facebook status or Tweet, quote that you see on Pinterest or other social media, a billboard that makes you stop and think, or any other piece of writing that causes you to reflect. Write about why you chose that piece of writing, its potential purpose and audience, its meaning, and the feelings evoked from the message. Most importantly, how does it speak to both you and the audience for which it was intended? Such relevant topics can quite easily be turned into a blog at some point, if you ever get to a place where you want to share your writing.

7. **Write about random thoughts that come to mind.** Instead of focusing on a certain topic, let your mind wander, see where it goes, and record those thoughts. This can be fun but also daunting. Do not concern yourself with the structure of the writing; instead, focus on the authenticity of the content. These can be the most interesting to read later on, since random thoughts have no agenda and can reveal a great deal about who a person is and what he or she is thinking about at any given time, especially when recorded over a span of time. Questions this journal might answer

are: a) What am I thinking right now at this moment? b) How am I feeling physically? Mentally? Emotionally? c) How are my thoughts connecting as I am sitting here?

8. **Choose a thought or feeling every week that you want to vent about.** Express your anger or pain if you need to. This type of journal can be a good tool for coping with depression, loss, or grief and can help you process the emotions you are feeling. The important concept to remember is to be completely honest in facing whatever it is you are facing. Do not try to sugarcoat the issues or write what you want people to think you are feeling. Remember this is your journal, and the agenda should be solely your own. Questions this journal might answer are: a) What is making me angry today/this week? b) What is making me sad, upset, or distraught? c) What emotions am I feeling? d) Why am I feeling them? e) What do I do with these feelings? f) How can I become more positive in this thought process?

9. **Begin a gratitude journal that causes you to be grateful for all that you have in your life.** This is another great tool for coping with depression as it forces writers to focus on the positive aspects of life, rather than dwelling on the negative emotions. Every day, write down one person, place, or thing for which you are grateful. Explain why you are grateful and what your life might be like without it. Focus on the qualities of that person, place, or thing that make such meaningful to you. Questions this journal might answer are: a) Who makes me happy? b) What material possessions do I have that most people do not? c) How is my physical health? d) What are the experiences that I get to enjoy that make me smile? e) What makes me special? f) What is one thing that I would miss if I were to be without it?

10. **Begin a goals journal where you set forth your goals in life.** Discuss each week what you are doing to attain those goals. Focus on the success you experience, even if it is not as great or as quick as you would like. Assign dates to those goals so that you can tangibly measure when and how they are attained. Dream big or focus small, depending on your personality and state of mind. The important thing is that you make yourself accountable for these goals and strive to attain them, if even by baby steps. You may surprise yourself at how far you can come when setting your mind to an objective. It is always a great idea to write down goals or objectives when possible as doing so encourages success. Questions this journal might answer are: a) What are my career or academic goals for this week/month/term/year? b) What are my physical goals for this week/month/term/year? c) What are my emotional or mental goals for this week/month/term/year? d) What are my spiritual goals for this week/month/term/year? e) What are my financial goals for this week/month/term/year? f) What are the steps I can take to achieve these goals? g) How can I chart my progress tangibly? h) What will happen if my goals are met? i) What will happen if these goals are not met?

11. **Write down the highlights and lowlights of each day/week/month.** This is similar to the kind of diary that many people keep or kept as children. Such writing focuses on the daily aspects of life that we would forget if we were not writing them down. This can be a good source for recording day-to-day life and can serve as a log for the daily events of your life on which you can reflect years later. It can describe events, accompanied by your thoughts and feelings associated with those events. Years later, these journals can help us recall events that otherwise might be long forgotten in the

recesses of our minds as we age. Questions this journal might answer are: a) What did I do today? b) Did I have any meaningful experiences? c) What are three words that describe my day? e) Has my day/week been a good one or bad one? Why?

12. **Write about what you are feeling at the moment. Unlike random thoughts, these types of entries focus on feelings.** You can, for example, title, "What I Am Feeling Today" or "My Thought for the Day". It doesn't need to be deep or profound; instead, again focus on the authenticity and integrity of the moment and what you are feeling. Reject the need to be politically correct. Journals are designed to be brutally honest and should reflect given thoughts and emotions at any given time in life. Questions these journals might answer are: a) What am I feeling today? b) Why am I feeling it? c) How does this feeling differ from what I was feeling yesterday?

13. **Write about an ongoing problem or social issue that is troubling to you.** It can be personal, communal, or global. Read as much as you can daily about that issue, and record and chart the progress, or lack thereof, in solving that issue. Questions this journal might ask and answer are: a) Are other people working to fix the issue? b) More importantly, is there anything I can do to help? c) What is actually being done to fix this issue?

14. **Write a prayer journal if you are a spiritual person and believe in a higher power.** If you belong to a certain religious group and there is a manual or book, such as the Bible, which serves as the foundation for this faith, record those passages that speak to you. Tell why they are important to you. Write prayers or meditations to God, to your higher power, which display love, worship, gratitude, or thanksgiving. Write about how He or it is working in your life. Record prayers of petition. Be real and transparent in your journal.

15. **Write a series of letters to people in your life to tell them how much they mean to you, or how much they hurt you, if that is the case**. You do **not** have to send these letters, unless you feel led, but often writing to people can help us realize just how much they mean to us. Doing so can also clarify misunderstandings or help us move past events that caused us hurt or pain. If you opt to send the letters, it is possible they will help other people feel appreciated or mend relationships that might be broken and in need of repair. Writing these letters may help us purge any kind of ill we are harboring toward individuals in our lives. The reality is that people who hold grudges or fail to forgive others are hurting themselves more than the people whom they cannot forgive.

16. **Write an inspirational journal.** This can be a journal that is written to motivate and inspire other people by sharing your experiences and advice. It can expose your vulnerabilities and struggles and also your victories and triumphs. It can serve as a self-help book for you and others as well.

If you are wanting to start a journal, hopefully one of the ideas I just described appeals to you and can serve as a starting point for you to begin the journaling process. The beneficial idea behind journals is that the only master you are serving in writing them is you. You can make your journal whatever you want, and although it is good to be consistent in theme or style, you do not always have to follow that. You can write a journal entry every day for the rest of your life and record even the smallest details or emotions that you want to savor. Again, this is your work, and you are the master.

Finally, I hope you have discovered some possible approaches that you can try with your writing project. The most difficult task is starting. From there, you just need to let your heart take over and the rest will follow.

Writing for Reflection

1. *If you could choose any piece of writing (either something you have already written or something you hope to write) that could be remembered long after you are gone, what would you choose?*

2. *If you could write a topic-related journal, what topic would you pick?*

3. *Write down one of your fondest memories as a child or young adult.*

4. *Write a short poem that describes what you feel today.*

5. *If you could write a novel, what would you call it? Describe the plot in brie*

6. *Choose something you read recently and respond to it.*

7. *What kind of journal sounds the most appealing to you?*

Being Real in Our Writing

Writing is Dependent on Where We are in Our Lives

Another aspect of writing to consider is that it will always be contingent upon our mood, our feelings, and our interactions with other people—in short, where we are emotionally, spiritually, and even physically at any given point in our life. What is going on in our life is going to affect our writing, every time, always.

Consider this scenario. You are working on a writing project, whether it be a short story, a blog, or even a novel. You are writing daily, and you have allotted yourself writing time in the evening, around 7 p.m. Scenario #1: That morning, you oversleep. You jump into your car, head to work without a shower, and you realize that the AC on your car is not working. It's 90 degrees today. You sweat on your 40- minute commute to work and arrive at your desk several minutes late. Your boss doesn't say anything, but you get the "look."

Your friend calls you and cancels your lunch, which is fine, but you realize that in your haste to get out the door, you forgot your wallet/purse. Since you thought you were going to lunch with your friend, you didn't bring your lunch. Now you have no money to eat. You ask a few co-workers for some cash, and you are able to find $10 for lunch. You head to your car, and just as you pull out of the company parking lot, you notice your gas gauge shows "empty." So, the $10 that you were able to mooch for lunch now has to be spent on gas or you won't get home. You go get your gas, return to work, and have a really bad rest of the day. You somehow make it home, realize that your significant other didn't make dinner as promised, and the kids are all bickering at you because there is nothing to eat. After scrambling some eggs and making some pancakes and patting yourself on the back for using the old "breakfast for dinner" saves-the-day routine to fill up hungry tummies, you finally sit down to write.

Scenario #2: It's Groundhog Day and you get to start the day over. You wake up ten minutes early after a 10-hour night of sleep. You decide to take an extra long shower and get up to see breakfast on the table, thanks to your 17-year-old daughter, who just wanted to do something nice for you. You eat a full breakfast, hop into your car, and arrive at work 20 minutes early.

You log in to find an email from your boss, congratulating you on an employee-of-the-month award, and a box of cupcakes lands on your desk, courtesy of a good friend. Your boss takes you to lunch, pays for the whole thing, and lets you take the rest of the afternoon off for a job well done. He gives you a gift card to your favorite department store. You get off of work early, stop off at the said department store, buy your favorite pair of lounging pants, and head home. Since you're early, you decide to make a great dinner, and afterward, your family decides to do the clean up while you go off to a quiet room to write.

Looking at these two scenarios, do you think that the writing you do after the first one is going to look like the second? Will there be a different tone? The answer to this is most certainly. How you feel at any given moment will affect both the quality and quantity of the words you write. It will also affect the tone and your creativity. Even though your writing in scenario #1 will be vastly different than scenario #2, both of these pieces are still likely going to be true to who you are. Obviously, however, one will likely be a bit more negative in tone, while the other will be more upbeat.

Recording these highs and lows in life is a great advantage to the journaling process. However, be prepared for changes in perspective and tone. True honest writing will be parallel to what is occurring in your life, so don't always think you have to write only when you are having a great day or only when you are feeling down. Write when you feel like writing, and even when you don't. Don't force it, and don't think that you have to write only when you are clear-headed and in charge of your emotions. In truth, many of your best thoughts might come to you in the middle of the night, driving your car on a long commute, or right before you are about ready to fall asleep.

Advantages to Honest Writing

As we journal, we might discover that there is something therapeutic in penning some of the thoughts that we often bury in the deepest crevices of our minds. Often we don't even recognize they are there until we pour them out on the screen of a computer or in the pages of a journal.

Expressing emotion through writing and writing to process can have many benefits. When we write as a means of processing, there are several advantages to this:

- We do not need to worry about pleasing anyone; therefore, our writing tends to be more honest. We can be more transparent with ourselves and perhaps face truths we might not otherwise face.
- We do not need to be bogged down by the formalities of writing.
- We don't need to worry about offending or hurting anyone. A blank screen or journal can handle anything we write, as opposed to people, who are human and will have some kind of reaction—good or bad—to our writing.
- We can chart our "progress" or lack thereof, in our journey. We can also monitor our feelings so we can see growth and restoration when the time comes.
- Our writing can, as I have shared, touch the lives of others who suddenly don't feel so alone when they read that we are going through or feeling the same emotions as we are.
- Our writing can help us focus on the positive aspects of our lives.
- Our writing can provide a legacy for our children and grandchildren.

- We might be able to better understand why we do what we do and feel what we feel.
- Our writing can be used as a tool for us to gain clarity or for perspectives to be revealed to us.
- Through our writing, we might feel closer to God if we are a person of faith by writing in such a way that verbal prayer doesn't always allow.

Expressing Both Negative and Positive Emotions

Another aspect to keep in mind as we journal is that we often might find ourselves surprised by all of the emotions that will emerge in print: some of them negative and some of them positive in nature. I hope you will experience both. We need to tell ourselves it is "okay" to express negative emotions, even if they might come in a very ugly form. Again, since we are the audience, we can handle it. We have trained ourselves since most of us live in a fish bowl due to social media, that we have to be politically correct, that we have to uphold a facade, and that we have to only express feelings and post ideas that will make us look "together" and happy. This concept of "keeping up with the Joneses" is not new: it has been around long before social media ever reared its multifaceted head. However, since we are constantly being barraged with how fabulous everyone else is right now, it puts additional pressure on us to express the same.

The comforting aspect of journaling is that it allows people a safe place to express themselves without that fish bowl mentality. We need to return to our roots of being real with ourselves. We need to take off our masks and be real with who we are and what we are going through.

As we journal, it is acceptable and encouraged to express those negative emotions—to delve deeply and honestly. However, we must not allow them to consume us. We need to use our journaling as a way to process and overcome. The law of contrary is a beautiful law of nature. It basically says that we cannot experience the positive in life without experiencing the negative. We cannot experience light without darkness; joy without pain; peace without strife; success without failure; Luke Skywalker without Darth Vader. Journaling shares this concept. It is only through recording our negative emotions that we can see the positive, and vice versa. In a nutshell, through this journey, we should confront the negative, but we should not be afraid to celebrate the positive.

Writing As a Process

Another facet of writing we need to establish is that writing is not a finite act: rather, it is a process with a defined beginning, but not a clearly defined end. If we take our writing to the next level and decide to share it with others, there will come a time when we may feel like it "is never good enough" or "needs more". We will want to rewrite and revise and think of things to add after we think we are actually finished. The famous quote, attributed to a number of free thinkers, "Done is better than perfect" most certainly applies to anything we write: journal or published article. As we begin writing, therefore, we must think of it as a process that may never truly end. We may happen upon the journal we begin today years from now and decide to add to it.

The beginning stage of writing anything—again formal or informal—involves the brainstorming stage. This is the stage where we determine our audience and purpose and begin to get our ideas, although unorganized and basic, down on paper or computer. I encourage writers to create bullet lists, free write, or draw cluster diagrams to get their thoughts out of their heads. The important thing is that the thoughts take form and become tangible for us and other readers.

Secondly, if our writing is going to end up as a coherent piece that is intended to be shared, we need to have a main idea that permeates what we write. If we are just free writing and journaling, this is not as important. However, if we want to share our writing later, we need to have a main idea; in formal writing, we call this a thesis. Everything we write as part of that piece should tie into that main idea. We need to keep that in mind as we write.

The third stage of writing involves revision. This can be one revision or ten. Again, this stage applies only to writing that is intended for an audience other than ourselves. Because writing is directly tied to our mood, this phase is very important, as what we write one day may not be what we feel the next. Have you ever, for example, written an email or message to a friend in anger and immediately regretted it within seconds of sending it? Or written a journal one day only to be shocked that you were feeling those emotions a few days later? Or found your diaries you kept as a teenager detailing your first "love" or your first date and were shocked at how smitten you were?

I have had all these experiences; they have taught me that writing is very much tied to our emotional states, and like those, can change from one day to the next. These have also taught me how powerful the written word can be (a point I made in the prologue) and why it is vital that we choose our words carefully, no matter who our audience is.

Writing for Reflection

1. *Is it hard for you to be completely honest when you write?*

2. *Describe a safe place in your life.*

3. *What are ways you cope with sadness or depression currently?*

4. *Discuss how writing can be one such coping mechanism for you.*

5. *Describe your own writing process, both for personal writing and other forms of writing that you will share (i.e. assignment, email, etc.).*

6. *Have you had an experience where you wrote something that you regretted sending to another person? What was the result?*

7. *Have you ever written something one day that surprised or shocked you when you read it later? Describe this experience.*

8. *Do you prefer to write when you are sad or happy? Would you be open to writing during times when you feel both emotions?*

The Need to Create

I am one of those people who admittedly always has to have a project list to get me up in the morning. I keep a detailed calendar that I update at the beginning of every week. I especially savor the feeling that comes when I can take one of my highlighters and cross something off my list for the day. Strangely, for me, there are very few things more satisfying than looking at my list for the day and seeing everything on it crossed off.

Admittedly, many of the items on my to-do list have to do with creation in some shape or form. Some of them are artistic in nature, such as the creation of a fiction work; creation of another writing course; creation of content for a newsletter; or creation of a journal entry. Other things are less so: creation of a new meal that I want to prepare or the creation of a more efficient way to feed my cats to prevent my big cat from stealing everyone else's food.

However, no matter what form it takes, I believe all of us are created to create, even if we are not necessarily talented in the areas where we ordinarily think of creativity. Even if we are not good writers, painters, singers, lyricists, poets, artists, or musicians, we still are likely to create something almost every day of our lives without realizing it. We cook and create meals for our families. We create new looks when we paint a room or remodel our homes. We create businesses to earn a living. We create reports or task lists for our jobs. We create little songs to remember things. We create school projects for our kids. We create "to do" lists for cleaning. We create grocery lists to stock our pantries. We create resourceful ways to earn extra income. We help our kids create lemonade stands in front of our homes. We create systems for the garage sale we are having on Saturday. We create dreams when we are slumbering. We create ways to bypass rules that we don't want to follow. I could go on and on, but you get the idea. Our human brains were made to create. Those of us who are wired creatively are even more at a disadvantage when we are stifled from creating.

As a teacher, if I was not undertaking some project on my semester breaks, I would have difficulty getting up each day. I found myself asking the "what-am-I-doing with my-life" deep questions, and I began to feel like I was wasting away, with no real purpose. Somewhere along the way, I figured out if I created a project over my break, those thoughts and feelings would subside. Sometimes the projects did include artistic writing endeavors or creation of content or videos. Other times, it was a more practical project, like organizing my basement or creating a book of recipes to make my cooking easier on my longer days in the heat of the semester.

Years ago, when the pandemic and subsequent quarantine hit, like many people, I began sinking into depression, finding my fast-faced, hectic lifestyle reduced to a mere crawl, sometimes with hours of time to fill. With my commute time reduced by 10-12 hours a week, my house organized, and no errands to run, I had difficulty, about three weeks into it, wondering how I was going to rebound. When I was forced to work online, I remember feeling like it was time to get a new career, although even that seemed overwhelming and daunting.

Eventually, I decided one day to pick up my computer and start writing a new novella—with the intent of only revisiting the craft and practicing skills I hadn't used in a very long time—at least not for that purpose. I ended up writing some 200 pages in two weeks and then started a second one. Suddenly, I found something I had lost for decades: the love of writing for the sake of writing. I wasn't writing to create a lesson or to be published; I was writing for the sole purpose of bringing something to life.

I relate this story because I firmly believe—even more so after talking with countless people in my boat—that having a creative endeavor can help those who are looking for purpose, who are facing the big life questions that have them searching for this purpose, and even those who simply want a means to propel them through the day. This can be even more meaningful if you are able to find a way to help other people in the process—others who might be feeling like they are alone in what they feel, others who might be feeling exactly what you are feeling.

Determine your Personality Type

Most of us have, at one point in our lives, taken a personality test, one that defines our personal traits, quirks, strengths, and weaknesses. Some of them even offer us tips on how to find careers that fit who we are or will make us more satisfied and fulfilled in our lives. I highly encourage you, if you have not already done so, to find one or more of these tests online, if nothing else so you can get a snapshot of who you are. While these tests may not always be accurate, many of them are spot on and could offer you life tips on how to approach your strengths and weaknesses. Most of these tests can also tell you if you have the type of personality that is more artistic and creative in nature. Typically, those of us who lean more toward the creative side also tend to be the ones who struggle most with introspection and depression. We are also empaths, which makes us more sensitive in general.

When it comes to personality tests, the Myers Briggs Foundation is the most common one that people take and for the most part is accurate at depicting the kind of person you are (given that you answer the questions honestly). Even Adobe has a brief one that will tell you what type of creative you are. I have found, in my case as well as the case of many others, that discovering a creative outlet, such as writing, could be exactly what you need in your life to fill a void that you have been otherwise unable to fill. At the minimum, it can help you learn to articulate what is going on in your head and put these thoughts into some kind of tangible form that you could potentially be able to share with friends, family, or therapists.

Power in Creation

There is power in the act of creation. Creation is the one aspect of your life over which you have complete control. Many other aspects of our life are definitely beyond our control, especially these external factors going on in the world today. Escaping into a world of our own creation has many benefits—again allowing us to have some control over one avenue of our lives. The important thing is to find a writing project or projects that excite you. The beautiful thing about writing is that there is absolutely no pressure from any direction, unless you create some for yourself. You can keep it as private as you want, so you can experiment and seek out new writing outlets that you may not have ever tried before.

Believe it or not, you can start something new or try a new hobby without announcing it to the entire world on social media. No one says that you have to tell your family and friends that you are undertaking a journal, a short story, poetry, or even on a grander scale, a novel. Given that we all spend an inordinate amount of time on our phones anyway, put down your phone and substitute that time with writing. Again, it doesn't need to be hours starting out. It can be just a few minutes a day. If you find that you want to keep writing, then keep going. I can almost guarantee that spending time writing in place of perusing the bad news in the media today will be far more rewarding and invigorating. It will also allow you to gain confidence in your skills that you may not otherwise be able to gain.

So to sum up, we all possess an innate power to create. Harnessing this power can open doors that we might not otherwise experience. It is up to us to take the steps to find out what it is that will give us purpose and could ultimately change our lives and the lives of others.

Writing for Reflection

1. *What are some things you hope to create?*

2. *Describe your own personality in a few sentences.*

3. *Do you find that you enjoy creative outlets, or do they stress you out?*

4. *On a less formal basis, in what ways do you create every day?*

5. *Do you tend to announce your creative endeavors when you start one? Why/ why not?*

All Aboard the Struggle Bus

We are going to start this lesson out by making a list. You can do this mentally or physically, but please take the time to seriously think about these two questions. First, think about a recent time(s) when you read something online that made you deliriously happy? Write it down or make a deliberate mental note of it. Secondly, now think about a recent time(s) when you read something online that made you feel sad, inadequate, hurt, depressed, angry, or left out. Write it down or make a deliberate note of it.

Chances are, especially given the current state of our entire planet (riots, hurricanes, quarantines, pandemics, and plagues) that the second list was probably easier and likely more plentiful than the first. We are living in troubled times, although I think each generation before us likely expressed similar sentiments.

One fact that might help you in these times, however, is that you need to remember that all of us—no matter how perfect or together we appear to be on the surface—are all imperfect; we are all flawed. We all have our struggles, our fears, our inadequacies, our vices, and our addictions. We all go to bed each night with worries and concerns that sometimes keep us awake more than asleep. We all have made bad decisions with even worse consequences.

When I was in graduate school, I read a story once that was pretty impactful, although now in trying to find the exact author and title, even Google has failed me. It tells the story of an anonymous note that was sent to townspeople in a small town. I know I am butchering the note, but it basically says something along the line of, "I know your secret. You need to leave town." Somehow, the note ends up being circulated among the townspeople. Before long, the entire town has been abandoned, each person thinking the note was directed toward them.

The plot of this story, embedded deep with irony, is that everyone in the small town had a secret to hide. I think the same would likely be true today, even in our fast-paced busy world of perfect selfies, perfect spouses, perfect kids, perfect jobs, and perfect vacations. We all have our dark side, our secrets, our mistakes, and our transgressions that we try to keep buried. Instead, we all have a desire to let the world see our best side. While there is absolutely nothing wrong with that to some degree (after all, who wants to see or know about our double chins and wrinkles; our kids in detention at school; our marital spat over laundry; our vacation in our five-story hotel that sported bed bugs and holes in the wall), it can be extremely discouraging to those on the other receiving end who feel like they can never measure up.

Studies are now starting to show the devastating consequences of this comparison syndrome. Depression and suicide are at an online high—some of which is being directly attributed to social media. Experts are even finding terms for some of this. We have all heard of the term, "Fomo" (fear of missing out), the phenomenon that occurs when people are glued to their phones and social media accounts because they think that they will miss out on something important. Even Instagram, which started out as a platform to share beautiful photos, is known to be a culprit in the depression war, according to recent studies. Thanks to the ease and use of selfie filters, it's easy to look stunning with a few swipes on the app.

Even the most secure and successful human being walking the earth can be made to feel inadequate after perusing social media and seeing how great the lives of everyone else can be. Social media has grown to be one of those necessary evils in our world today. If we are not on social media, we tend to miss out on important world events, births, deaths, community garage sales, and other important family events that people don't take the time to share with us personally anymore. It is sad when we read news on social media more quickly than we hear about events from our family and friends who should be making a phone call. Even text messages are more personal than social media, where the whole world is apt to see events that shape our lives even before we are.

Social media has in many ways done the exact opposite of what it was intended to do. Yes, granted, when used correctly, it connects people. We are able to reconnect with long lost friends we haven't seen in years, keep up with the number of kids our good friends are having, and see when someone we cared about has passed away. Before the days of social media, we had to look them up in a phone book and call them or meet them for lunch or coffee! Or by accident when we ran into them at the grocery store of the town where we grew up. However, in our honest moments, we have to admit, even the most diehard of us who are addicted to our online accounts like drug addicts on meth, that social media has made us a bunch of insecure people who gain affirmation, recognition, and even acceptance from the numerous "likes," "comments," "retweets", "favorites," and emoticons that people add to show us they took the time to think about us, if only for a second.

Sadly, social media has replaced human interaction, from phone calls to dates, to walks in the park, and there is likely little that can be done to change what we have become. That being said, we also have to admit that most people, in their brutally honest moments, do not feel good about their own lives after spending hours scanning through Facebook, Instagram, or Snapchat, and others yet to come. The comparison trap is all too alive and well, and we all fall prey to it at one time or another. One way to avoid this comparison trap is to put down the phone and focus on other
projects. This week's prompts will all relate to what I call becoming a "seeker" of other projects, rather than what is taking place on your phone.

First, seek ways to help others. Step outside of yourself, of your reaction to what is   happening in the world, and assign yourself a project that is important to your little corner of the world.

- Look for ways to incorporate random acts of kindness into your life. Go out of your way to deliberately do something nice for someone. At the minimum, smile at a stranger, who just might be feeling what you are feeling or worse. Then write about it.
- Look for ways to serve those who have it worse off than we do. There are always those people out there who are worse off, even if we feel like we are in the bottom of the pit. Seek out those people and find ways to make a difference in their lives. These could be people in your own circles or strangers you have never met. Write about it.
- If you are able and have never owned a pet, pour your time and energy into a furry friend. I have seen many success stories of people who were at their lowest point in their lives and adopted a dog or cat or ferret or bird, or even a chicken; and turned their lives around by giving themselves to another living being who depended entirely on them. There is something about having a sense of responsibility that can often lift us out of the trenches of what we are going through. Write about it.

Second, seek creative outlets. Beginning a creative endeavor can honestly be one of the best treats you can give yourself. Even if it is simply to record what you are going through every day, having that sense of accomplishing something and gaining perspective through writing can be a great way to start creating a sense of discipline in your own life. The main thing is that no matter what creative outlet you seek, make it a positive experience. Force yourself to see things from a brighter perspective. Force yourself to slow down and do something productive.

A final note in this lesson is that we all need to realize that we are not alone. Somewhere in some corner of the world, someone is likely experiencing some of the same feelings that we are experiencing. They are likely facing some of the same life challenges and going through some of the same experiences. That is why writing is so important: it connects us to others in ways other experiences cannot. Many people are afraid to speak up in a group or admit a shortcoming out loud, but they will do so when given pen and paper, or a keyboard and a computer screen. Writing can truly connect people.

If you have time to read, think about the characters you encounter in books. Or think about the actors you see in movies or in a series you watch. The fictional world has a way of helping us empathize with others, to feel what they are feeling, to see life through their perspective. To sum up, that is the beauty of writing: it helps us see that we are not alone, that we all have ridden, at one time or another, on the struggle bus, and we can all help each other through these ups and downs of life. The pen—or the keyboard—can be a beautiful way of bridging that emotional gap between us and other people. We just have to reach out and write.

Writing for Reflection

1. *How much interaction do you have with social media, if any? What is your perception of it?*

2. *Keep track for a day how much time you spend on your phone. Discuss this.*

3. *Why do you think we as humans are so inherently wired to feel like we need to keep up with our peers? Do you find yourself falling into this trap?*

4. *When you do spend time on your phone, how does it generally make you feel?*

5. *What are some ways you can refocus your energy onto more positive outlets?*

6. *Do you find yourself comparing yourself to others? If so, how can you change your mindset to make this more healthy?*

Determining your Project and Your Purpose

One of the most exciting yet most daunting aspects of becoming a writer is the selection of a project to begin. In short, you know that you want to write. Now, you just need to decide on what you want to write. Beyond the prompts and the ideas for the journals listed in the early lesson, here are some suggestions that I encourage people to explore as they begin their writing journey.

Brainstorm. Keep an ideas journal handy. It is important to have an ideas journal that you keep separate from your main journal. This can serve as a repertoire of ideas that you can use to begin and continue your writing projects. I encourage people to divide this journal into "Small Project Ideas" and "Big Project Ideas" headings. If it is an idea for a journal or a fleeting thought that you might want to explore at some point in the future, write it in the "Small Project" list. If it is more along the lines of a short story or even bigger—a blog or book idea, you can write it in the "Big Project" list. Keep this idea journal handy, especially at night or rest when many good ideas come to writers. Write down these ideas whenever you have them, not just at a select time when you are forcing yourself to brainstorm, although this is okay too.

You can get these ideas from anywhere: other works you have written or read, online, media posts, writing groups, random thoughts that come to mind, billboards—just about anyplace where ideas can come to life. This is more or less, the brainstorming process, and as a life-long writer, this process can take place at any time, anywhere. It can take 30 seconds or 30 minutes, depending on how quickly and thoroughly the ideas come to mind.

If you have no idea where to start, then start with writing prompts. In general, writing begets more writing. The more you write, the more ideas for future writing endeavors will begin to emerge. The main thing is to get the project—any project—going. Let the rest fall. At some point, you do need to make the decision as to whether the crux of your writing will be geared toward fiction or nonfiction writing projects, or a combination of both. Are you going to stick with a journal, or at some point, do you want to branch out and undertake a fiction piece? It doesn't have to be the massive undertaking of a novel; it can be a short story or even a poem.

Start small. While it is easy to want to establish high and lofty goals as a writer, it is best to start small and focus on shorter and less intimidating projects, such as this study, which can be completed within a shorter time frame. Journal entries are a very easy way to build the habit of writing into your everyday life. Poetry is another easy way to get started. If, at some point, you want to graduate to more involved projects such as short fiction stories, self-help articles, blog posts, or informative articles for print or web, those can be less daunting but still provide a sense of accomplishment. They can also help you realize if you want to break into the world of freelance writing. Or they can be added to a writing portfolio that you can store for the future. At the very minimum, they can help you focus on the craft of writing and find out what you enjoy and what types of writing endeavors are not your idea of a good writing day.

If after completing a few manageable projects, you want to set your sights on a more involved and intense project, such as a self-help book or fiction adventure story, then have at it. There is nothing quite as exciting as a writer to begin such a vast undertaking. Keep in mind, however, that you need to establish discipline if you are going to succeed in any long-term writing project.

Focus on one project from that list at a time. Once you have created an Ideas Journal, choose one of the projects from that list to begin. Do not try to switch things up in the beginning. It is easier to focus on one project at a time. As a creative, if I allowed myself to, I could have 18 different projects going simultaneously. That is no joke, which you will realize if you embrace writing as a lifestyle. I have to rein myself in and focus on one project at a time. It is best to finish one project before beginning another one. It will build discipline and follow through. It will also instill a sense of success at the end of the day. It can become very frustrating and disheartening to have multiple projects that have been started but none that are complete. Even if you have no intention of sharing what you have written, it is important to finish a project before starting another one.

Switch it up. Finally, as a long-term, lifestyle writer, it is important that you try new things and learn to switch things up. Try your hand at different genres, different points of view, different tenses, and different means of organization. Try some short projects and longer ones. Try collaboration when the opportunity arises. Do not limit yourself. Like anything if you want to grow or get better at something, you have to do it often and you have to practice—a lot.

Determine your purpose. Any project we undertake in your life, any career we choose, or any relationship we begin all have something very innate in common, even if we do not consciously think about it: they all have a purpose. We may not write it down or tell anyone; we may not even realize it, but everything we set out to do or spend our time doing has a purpose behind it. We eat to sustain our bodies; we exercise to get healthy or lose weight; we begin a relationship to find fulfillment and seek companionship; we buy a house to have a place to eat, drink, and sleep. We go through a drive through to satisfy a craving; we look at our phones to get information or to satisfy an addiction. So it is with writing.

Everything we write has a purpose behind it. Most of these purposes, which were discussed early on, are academic: we write to entertain, to persuade, and to inform. As also stated in earlier lessons, we can also write to process. Sometimes, the writing project we undertake seeks to fulfill one of these purposes; other projects may fill a couple of purposes. Then there is the rare project that may fulfill all four, even if that was not its original intent.

Our first task in beginning your project is to determine your purpose. In doing so, you need to ask yourself these basic questions:

1. Why am I going to begin this writing project?
2. What do I hope to accomplish upon completion of this project?
3. Do I want to share this writing with other people?
4. Am I writing to entertain myself or others?
5. Am I writing to share my perspective or inform someone of information of which they may not be aware?
6. Am I writing to persuade someone to accept a belief or idea or to at least consider my point of view?
7. Am I writing simply to process what I am feeling?
8. Am I writing to create? Am I writing to escape?

Having a purpose will definitely play a huge role in so many aspects of your writing, including the following:

1. **The format you choose.** If you are writing to persuade, inform, or entertain, then obviously it is best to put your writing into electronic form to start with it; that way, it will be easy to pass along to others when the time comes for you to do that. If, on the other hand, you are writing for the sole purpose of processing and have no desire to share your information with any other audience, the format you choose to write could be very simple. Since there will be no need to disseminate the information, you can write in a journal or notebook. Even if you plan on sharing it later, you can still use pen and paper. It can always be converted to an electronic form, although this will be tedious and take some time to type the content out onto a computer. As with all things electronic, there are some risks associated with putting everything on a computer. Especially if your writing is deeply personal, it can fall prey to probing eyes or easy dissemination. If someone, through purpose or happenstance, finds your writing, it is easy to cut and paste, forward, or share something with the click of a mouse. I always encourage people who are going to use electronic means to journal or share private thoughts to put a passcode on the file, which can be easily done through most word-processing programs. That way, if the file is accidentally discovered or shared, it will take some work to open it. Similarly, even notebooks or journals can also be discovered or found, but those cannot be as easily passed around or forwarded. Knowing your format before you begin writing can save you a lot of time, effort, and stress in the long run.

2. **The vocabulary you choose.** We all know that the words we use in our everyday life almost always depend on our audience. We will be discussing the audience in the next lesson in this regard. However, as with the audience, the purpose of our writing will heavily influence the vocabulary we use, and the style we use to share it. If we are again, writing solely for our eyes only, we do not need to concern ourselves with coherent, strong vocabulary, as the message is going to be more important than the

means. If our journal is meant for our eyes only, or for review years later, it doesn't matter if we use longer, more formal vocabulary that indicates a level of literacy or education. On the other hand, if we are going to share the work, we need to be aware of the words we use and the way we choose to use them. Profanity and clichés are usually discouraged in formal writing as often they can muddy the waters and distort the message. They can also create bias or even alienate your reader.

3. **The sensitivity level you choose.** Again, if we are writing to process only, then we do not need to concern ourselves with the feelings of others. We can be honest with what we are going through and have no regard for what others might feel if they were to read it. Although as with anything in life, if others do read our writing, they will form some opinion of us, even if they do not know us personally. It is something that is very prevalent, especially in today's world. If, on the other hand, our purpose is to share what we are writing, we need to be cognizant of how others might perceive what we are writing. Even though people are increasingly hateful online these days, deep down, they are easily offended. When the tables are turned, even if they have no regard for others, they do not like when others insult them. If your purpose is something other than to process, you are putting yourself at risk of alienating your audience and your message if you choose to be insensitive to their experiences and needs.

4. **The audience you choose.** Obviously, the audience we choose will be determined in large part first by our purpose. If we are writing to process, the audience of one, Me, is not going to be as difficult to please. If again, however, we are writing for a greater purpose, then the audience will definitely play a role in this.

5. **The sentence structure, grammar, and syntax you choose.** Just like vocabulary, if we are writing for the purpose of sharing our works with others, we will need to be aware of the sentence structure, grammar, and syntax we use when we write. Our writing will need to be more formal and educated; otherwise, again, judgment sadly will be cast upon us. If your purpose is to influence others, you can't just throw all conventions aside. Your message will only be as effective as the channel you choose to share. Think about the number of people in the throes of a hot debate, even on something as informal as social media, who get discounted because of their incorrect grammar or typos, which are almost always pointed as a last resort to demean someone. I see it over and over again. They get called illiterate or stupid, even though that may be far from the case—even if they are making valid points. If your purpose really is to influence, then you need to be aware of writing correct, formal English, if not initially, then in the final stages of revision before the writing is shared.

6. **The delivery method you choose to share, if this is the case.** If your purpose is to entertain, inform, persuade, or inspire, then you will need to be aware of the means you are hoping to share your work. This purpose will definitely impact how you plan to deliver it, whether it is a book, a blog, or some other public means of sharing. This should be determined early in the writing process, again, to save time and work later.

As we have seen, determining our project and our purpose is no small task, but doing so is important as we embrace writing as a lifestyle. Begin by writing in your Ideas Journal. Hopefully, out of that, you will be able to determine both your project or your purpose

Writing for Reflection

1. *Brainstorm for 10 minutes on potential projects you could begin.*

2. *Are you more excited about the idea of writing nonfiction or fiction?*

3. *When you begin any project, discuss the process whereby you ensure its completion.*

4. *Do you have a hard time completing what you start? If so, what obstacles do you face? If not, why are you successful?*

5. *From your list, choose one potential project that you would like to begin. Write about that project.*

6. *What would the purpose of this project be?*

Determining your Audience

After you determine your purpose, the next step is to determine your audience. The communication process, whether written or spoken, has several vital components to make it work correctly. Obviously, there is the originator of the message—the speaker or the writer—which is you. Then there is the message—your content—that is shared through the channel of communication, which in your case, is the written word. However, if the process were to stop here, your purpose in writing beyond would be null and void. Without the receiver of the communication—the audience—the process is incomplete. Even if the audience is yourself a few years down the line or yourself when you go back and read what you just wrote, the last part of that communication has to take place for the circle to be complete.

Your audience can range from super intimate (you) to a vast market (the public). The more intimate the audience, the less you have to concern yourself with many aspects of writing that professional writers have to think about, including facets we have already talked about (vocabulary, style, sensitivity, etc.). The greater and diverse your audience, the more care and concern need to go into analyzing the receivers of your information.

The Most Intimate Audience: You

If you are writing with the sole purpose of journaling, this part is easy. You are writing for an audience of a grand total of one: You. There is no easier writing project than this. If you are the audience, then you do not have to worry about any aspect of your writing whatsoever. You can be and are encouraged to be as honest and transparent as you possibly can. It is amazingly refreshing and therapeutic to go back and read what you wrote in a different time, even if it is just a few hours after you wrote it.

Again, as pointed out, there is always a concern as to the consequences of what will arise if another person, friend or foe, happens upon your private thoughts. However, as long as you take steps to protect that (i.e. lock up your written journal, passcode protect your files), the less likely this will occur. One word of caution, however, is that if you use a medium that is accessible by the web, such as Google docs, you must always be aware that there is a chance that someone can access your information. Experts who caution that anything put on the web is, more or less, permanent, are right on. What is put on the web always has the risk of being discovered. For that reason, I encourage people who want to delve into very private journaling to keep things either in written form or on a personal device that does not have web capabilities.

You + Those in Your Circle

I have worked with several authors now who have created their journals or memoirs to record their thoughts with the hope that someday these can be passed on to members of their family (i.e. kids, grandkids, etc.). In other words, while the journals are deeply private at the time they were written, the authors of these are writing with the intent of them being shared or discovered by family members, either later in their lives or after they have passed on. If you are one of those people, again, you must always look at the context in which these pieces of writing can be discovered. Realize that each generation lives in its own time bubble, and while many themes and experiences are somewhat universal in nature, others are not. It would be, for example, very difficult for someone born in today's world to understand what it was like growing up in the Great Depression, when money was scarce and technology as we know it was nonexistent. I have noticed even a vast difference between the era in which I grew up and the era in which I raised my own kids. If you are going to write for future generations, you must keep in mind that the world will change in leaps and bounds moving forward, and what might be true today might not be so in the future. You need to be aware of the need to explain things in depth if your goal is to get people to understand what you were feeling and experiencing in this season of your life.

A Specific Audience

If you have come to the place where you are interested in sharing your writing with a certain segment of the population (i.e. a target audience that might have something in common with your own experiences), you must be sensitive to the needs of this audience. Keep in mind that while you may share visions or goals with this specific audience, your experiences may not be theirs entirely, and you have to be aware of their wants, needs, and limitations. You must always be respectful and cognizant of others. Depending on your familiarity with this target audience, while you may have many things in common with them, you may not know all there is to know about their backgrounds. Everyone has a unique perspective, and all too often, we have tunnel vision and can only see life through our own me-centered glasses. This is in many ways what is entirely wrong with the world. If we have no real experience with what is going on around us, often we fail to realize its importance.

During the pandemic years ago, I was standing in a supermarket line, listening to a woman trying to talk an employee into removing his mask to breathe easier. She said the virus was a hoax and all hype and that masks were completely unnecessary. She of course was not wearing a mask. The gentleman behind her, who was wearing a mask, with all due respect, related that he had several work colleagues (within 30 miles of this supermarket) who had suffered from the virus, one of whom had died. He told her with great kindness that the virus was indeed not a hoax and most certainly not all hype, and that he hoped that she would never suffer its wrath. It was as his friend described, "the most horrible illness he had ever experienced in [his life]". If you are writing to share, you must always remember the famed quote spoken by Atticus, in Harper Lee's *To Kill a Mockingbird,* "You never really understand a person until you consider things from his point of view... until you climb into his skin and walk around in it." If you want to truly make an impact with your audience, you must always keep this in mind.

Public Consumption

If you have decided to officially go public with your writing, in the form of a blog or book, for example, you are setting yourself up for the harshest and most difficult audience: the public. The "public" nowadays is so open-ended that the person reading your work can be anyone, anywhere, at any time. It could be someone in the United States of America or someone in the heart of an African jungle who happens to be one of the lucky ones with Internet access. It could be a wealthy, esteemed celebrity or a person serving time behind bars for a crime he or she committed. It could be someone reading your work tomorrow or someone reading your work 50 or even 100 years from now. Knowing this, you must take into account all aspects of a person: their gender, their race, their nationality, their sexual orientation, their religion, their socioeconomic status, their language, their weight, their mental or physical limitations, and their life experiences that make them unique.

So many times in our society today, we overlook all of these aspects. We blurt out a comment or type a response on a post, not realizing that the words we wield will either build a person up or tear them down. There are few "in-betweens" in this regard. Almost every encounter we have with someone, if we give it true, rational thought, is either positive or negative, in some way. It either makes us feel happy or sad. Granted, there can be such a thing as a neutral encounter with a stranger in an elevator, for example. However, for the most part, if we have communication with someone, we come away with some kind of response. The pen (or keyboard) is indeed mightier in the sword, and all you have to do is scroll through social media to see this.

More often than not today, people online lock onto their First Amendment rights, not caring if they appear uneducated, biased, or downright crazy. It's all about expressing their own opinions, with, so often, very little sound reasoning to support their views. I have seen entire families split apart, all due to "freedom of speech" and the consequences of upholding that right. While this is one of the great gifts we get to receive living in the free world, we need to realize that we should not celebrate it with complete abandon—at least without not some kind of consequences taking place. If we want to impact an audience, we must utilize certain appeals in our writing to establish ourselves as credible, relatable, compassionate writers.

In persuasive writing, we call these the appeals, pathos, ethos, and logos, all Latin terms. Each of these appeals plays into our ability to relate to an audience. All of these together make us a strong writer. Pathos refers to the emotional response our writing can evoke in our reader. We use this appeal to try to get our readers to feel some kind of emotion, whether it be sadness, anger, or joy, or any emotion in between. Ethos refers to the credibility we establish with our readers. In other words, if we establish ethos, we demonstrate to our readers that we are believable and credible—that we know what we are talking about. Logos refers to reason, or logic, which one would think would be a pretty strong appeal in our world today. However, so many times, this goes out the window when people lock onto the emotional side of the argument, especially if someone has been offended.

If you want to truly connect with your audience and resonate with your audience, you have to establish as a writer that you care about them, even if you may not always agree with them or they may not always agree with your point of view. You must always keep your audience in mind.

Your Audience Determines Every Aspect of Your Writing

Just as in the purpose of writing, your choice of the audience impacts many aspects of your writing. The words you use, the style of your writing, the formality of what you write, the point of view from which you write—and so much more—all will be affected by your audience.

Think about it like this. If you were going to write a text to three different people—your spouse/partner, your boss, and a person in a writer's group—the vocabulary words you choose and the formality of your writing will all vary in these three instances. Generally speaking, you will use less formal writing with those who are closer to you, and more formal writing and vocabulary with those with whom you are less familiar or those in authority. It's the nature of writing. Sometimes, if we have a different or more specific purpose in mind, this may change; however, for the most part, the audience will determine more aspects of our writing than we realize.

In summary, we must never lose sight of our audience when we write. If you want to achieve your purpose, you must take the steps necessary to relate to them and certainly do everything in your power not to alienate them. I am not saying that you should not be free to express yourself; in fact, written expression is a powerful tool that often yields more results than other forms of communication. However, we must recognize the power that we have in sharing and realize that the communication process cannot be complete without our audience.

Writing for Reflection

1. *Who is your audience for the majority of your projects?*

2. *Have you ever reflected on anything you have written in the past? If so, what did you feel when you re-read it? If not, why is it that you have not?*

3. *Do you feel comfortable with those in your intimate circle reading your work? Why/why not?*

4. *If you had to target your writing for a specific audience, who would that audience be?*

5. *Have you considered writing and publishing something (besides every-day media posts) for the general public? How does this make you feel?*

6. *Have you experienced a loss of someone in your life due to something that was written or shared?*

7. *Have you ever been offended because a writer did not take your views or experiences into consideration? How did that make you feel?*

8. *Have you ever offended someone by something you wrote because you failed to take into account your audience? Discuss that experience. What was the end result?*

Determining your Goals

Now that you have an idea as to why you want to write, who you want to write for, and what you want to write, it is time to set a plan in motion to accomplish that. Even if you have the framework set, the journey is really just beginning.

First off, you need to determine your goals and put them in a tangible format so that you can meet them in a manner in which you are comfortable. You have to determine these early on in the process. Here are the initial main goals you need to determine as you begin this project.

1. *Time devoted to projects.* You need to decide how much time a week you can devote to your project. This is paramount if you want to succeed in any creative endeavor. Like any other major undertaking in our lives, if you do not build in time to accomplish something, it will always remain a distant bucket list item, something you will do when you have time or when you retire. Yet, how many people were given the unexpected leisure time due to the initial onset of the pandemic and found themselves bored and unable to start—let alone finish—any items on their bucket list? It's a human tendency. There is a certain inertia that exists in all of when it comes time to begin a project that is overwhelming and/or uncertain. It's hard to start something new. The first step is setting a goal that you can live with. You need to decide on a timed goal and stick with it.
2. *Word or page count goals.* If you are more of a numbers person, you can also set a writing goal of so many words or pages per day. Due to the wonderful age of technology in which we live, it is easy to record exactly how many words we accomplish on any given task. You can play around with this initially and find out what is a good target for you that will keep you engaged, yet not become too unrealistic. It might be 100 words or one page a day. Start small, so you don't set yourself up for failure. The important thing is that you set a goal that can be reached and improved upon the more disciplined you become as a writer.
3. *If you have a finite project, you absolutely need to give yourself a deadline.* You may tweak this as the need arises, but you have to start somewhere. Most of us, myself included, are procrastinators by nature. If we don't set a deadline, then the tendency is to put off tomorrow what we could do today. Even if you are undertaking an ongoing project, such as a journal, newsletter, or blog, then you can still set tangible deadlines (i.e. 52 entries by the end of 2021; 12 blogs (one per month) by the end of 2021; 52 newsletters by the end of 2021, etc.)

So what are the ways to solidify these writing goals? Here are the four approaches I recommend for developing a long-term habit of undertaking a writing project.

The Daily Goal

The first approach is to set yourself daily milestones, regardless of whether they are time-related or length-related goals. Optimally, if you can squeeze in about thirty minutes or so a day (a bit less if you are a fast typist), this is the best approach. You may be able to do it first thing in the morning or the last thing at night. Or perhaps you can make it a lunchtime activity.

Again, if you are better with finite word counts, then you can create a goal that centers on word or page counts. You can start with 500 words a day or 1-2 pages of writing a day, depending on the project. Stick with these goals as best you can, and do not make excuses for not meeting them. Whatever the case, writing a page of words a day will keep you on track to create discipline and achieve your goals. However, it has to become a daily habit, and it has to be every day. No matter what. If you miss a day and want to stay on track, then you will need to build in time to make it up another day, which is doable for most people, unless you work several jobs and have a family. It is important that you keep a record of your accomplishments each day; it will serve both as a motivator and recorder of your progress.

Although accounts vary, many experts on behavior psychology agree that creating a habit takes at least 21 days (some say more). So once you create this habit, it will become a part of your routine, like working out, eating, and going to work. If you miss a day, you might even feel lost, like your day isn't complete, and that is a wonderful feeling. It shows that you have the discipline to stay with it and to make your dream a reality.

The Weekly Schedule

Maybe you are a professional who works three days a week or four days a week, and then has a group of days off. Maybe you have some days or weekends where you are running from sun-up to sundown and can't squeeze in any extra activities other than sleeping, going to work, and eating. If this is the case, if your lifestyle is unpredictable, then it might be best for you to adhere to a weekly goal. Maybe you can choose to work every other day for thirty minutes or give yourself a whole day a week to write as much as you can. If it is word count or page count goals that drive you, then perhaps five pages a week would be a good starting point. Again, if your focus is on your weekly goal, then it doesn't matter when or how long you write, just as long as you hit this weekly goal consistently.

The Monthly Schedule

If daily or weekly writing goals create too much pressure for you, then it might be best for you to stick with a monthly writing goal. Again, your timing is all up to you, depending on the type of personality you have and what kind of time you can give. Some people do better writing in large blocks of time, a day off, for example, and if you can spare an entire day off one day a month to write, you can get quite a bit accomplished in that time frame. Or you can pick and choose your days that you want to write and break down the goal accordingly. A good page goal count per month is about 25-30 pages, given on average you would be writing a page a day.

Writing Retreats/Intensives

If your schedule is just too hectic and writing on a consistent daily, weekly, or monthly basis is too overwhelming for you, yet you still want to make writing a significant part of your life, you can schedule a few writing retreats or conferences per year. I know various writers who do this. They do a search for the type of conference or retreat they want at the beginning of each year, explore their options, register, and use those times to stay on track with their writing projects. This may be as little as one retreat per year or several, depending on time and budget constraints. The main thing, again, is to create a goal that is both feasible and manageable for you to meet. Setting yourself up with too high of expectations is a surefire way to kill any success or motivation you may have going into this project.

 **Writing for Reflection**

1. *In regard to your writing goals, are you more of a time person or a numbers person (would you rather center your goals around length of time writing or word count)?*

2. *Are you more comfortable with a daily, weekly, or monthly writing goal? Explain.*

3. *List out two different goals for your writing (i.e. word count/time devoted to writing per day/week/month): one that is manageable/feasible and perhaps one that is a little loftier. Explain the disparity.*

4. *If you could create the perfect writing retreat, discuss how it would be run.*

Creating Discipline

Now that you have decided on a set of writing goals, it will be of no value to you if you don't stick with it. Sticking with it entails creating a mindset, and this is perhaps the hardest step in this process. If you want to create discipline, in the beginning, it might be good to see writing as a work deadline so that you force yourself to meet it. You can give yourself some flexibility with the timing that you use, but it is vital that you meet your deadline. If you procrastinate and think, "Oh, I can make it up next week, or next month", that is where you will get into trouble.

The I-Can-Do-It-Tomorrow Attitude is the main reason why so many would-be writers don't ever get past the idea stage. Procrastination on any level is the kiss of death for any project. We all have a habit of putting off what we can do today, and starting a writing project is one of those goals that most of us put off, thinking we have all the time in the world to complete it. Before long, time gets away from us, and before we know it, another year has passed and we are no closer to beginning our project than we were when we first had the idea.

It requires us arriving at a certain place where we are tired of thinking about it, tired of telling others about it, and tired of sounding like a broken record and having others in our lives, look at us, and say, "yeah, yeah, yeah" as if they know we will never do it. How many people do we know who go on social media every day proclaiming they are going to start a new exercise routine, go back to school, or undertake some other lengthy and meaningful endeavor, only to be met with the inability to keep at it several days or weeks into their goal? They start out with the best of intentions, but everyday life gets in the way and prevents them from getting to the finish line.

Everyday life is probably the biggest hurdle to completing any writing project. In fact, everyday life is the biggest hurdle to accomplishing many of our dreams. Most of us have to go to a job to keep food on the table and a roof over our heads; since writing a dream book likely won't meet those two basic needs, we don't have a choice in the matter. So, by the time we go to work, eat a couple of meals a day, spend time with our loved ones, do the laundry, pay bills, and sleep, there isn't much time for anything else. To make it even more overwhelming and difficult, writing is a creative process that requires mental energy and stamina and a great deal of thought, even if we already have the ideas in our head. Many writers miss their self-imposed deadlines because by the time they get home at night, eat dinner, and spend time with their families, they are too tired to do anything else but sit on the couch—let alone undertake an activity that will force them to think. Hence, why so many people start a writing project and then drop off well before they are even close to making it a habit.

The Procrastination Traps

What are the traps that will prevent you from success? First off, like anything else, you recognize them. There are several traps—several mindsets—that you will fall into that will prevent you from staying on track.

The Justification Trap. The first is the justification trap. You will justify in your head in a million different ways why you haven't written in a few days, why you are behind, why you are not on track. It's a human tendency to justify our actions when we know we aren't doing what we should be doing. Remember, this is your goal, your dream, and you are in charge. You don't need to justify anything to anyone, even if you feel like you need to. Expending energy trying to come up with excuses why you are not writing takes just as much time as sitting down and writing. So, when and if you start doing this, stop, and start writing again.

The It's-Hopeless Trap. The second mindset that gets us into trouble is that our goals are so far off, so unattainable that it's hopeless. It's tough to discipline yourself when the payoff is only a few pages here, a few pages there. But like most things in life, anything with a huge payoff takes work, energy, and time. So on those days when you feel like you are never going to get there, realize you can and you will. The only hurdle preventing it from happening is you.

The Victim Trap. The third mindset that prevents us from accomplishing our goal is the victim mentality. As a teacher, I could write an entire book on all the excuses that students give why they aren't doing their work. Most of them also don't think it's their fault that they are failing. It's their parents, their spouses, their bosses, their significant others that dumped them, even their dogs. Many times, while these reasons can have some degree of truth, they are not what is keeping someone from success. Again, we can attain anything if we truly want it. That is one of the realities of life. We find the time, the money, or the means if we truly want something or someone. We will do what we need to do to get it. New parents, deprived of sleep, still get up eight times a night with a newborn, if they have to. Unemployed people still find ways to keep their lights on and food in their cupboards, even if it's tough and they have to sacrifice other things.

You have to want to write. You have to want to journal. You have to want to tell your story. If you truly want it, your school schedule, your job, your family won't get in the way. You will find the time to make it happen. We have a tendency to feel sorry for ourselves when someone or something prevents us from doing what we set out to do. The tragedy is that once you fall into the victim role, it's tough to get out of it. If you tell yourself you can't write because of other people or obstacles in your life and that it's not your fault, then the truth is you won't write. You have set yourself up for failure, and ironically, while you can blame anyone else you want, the truth is that it truly is your own fault. Don't be that person on social media or in your social circle who has a laundry list of dreams but doesn't accomplish any of them because of everybody and everything else.

The Unexpected Trap. The fourth and final mindset that will keep you from your writing goals is the something-unexpected-came-up-and-threw-me-off-track reality. You realize there are going to be a million different distractions that could pull you off course from writing. Some of these will be important—some of them will be unavoidable. They won't fall into the excuses category. They are going to be real-life bona fide issues that take your time and energy away from writing. You experience death or depression. You get married. You become ill. You start a new job. You have a child. You start dating the love of your life. You lose your job. You lose your best friend. You get dumped. Life happens every day, and there are times we don't have control of what is happening around us. Our train gets derailed, and there isn't a lot we can do to stop it.

Overcoming These Traps

So what do we do when we really do get derailed in our writing, either by these traps or real-life circumstances? The first step, like any step in solving a problem, is to recognize them and recognize them. Once you do that, there are two approaches you can take.

Take a break. The first approach is to simply take a break. Take time off. If you find yourself in this place and are thrown off course for a bit, the important thing is that you get back on as soon as you possibly can. If you have to work overtime for a job for a few weeks, have a looming school deadline. If you have a family issue that needs your immediate concern, realize it is okay to take a step back, to take a few days, or even weeks, off. A warning there, though: taking time off can be devastating for people who are routine-driven, especially when it comes to something like writing. If you take a day or month off from your schedule, whatever schedule that may be, you need to force yourself to get back on it and make up for lost time. That is why some people start but never finish. They are determined and excited to undertake the project in the beginning, but when they experience a setback, they lose all of their will to finish. And that is where discipline once again comes in.

Undertaking a writing endeavor is like an exercise regiment. Many of us decide, usually at the beginning of a new year, to make a resolution to get fit, exercise regularly, and eat healthier. So, we start a rigorous daily form of exercise, make a public announcement on social media, and set out with fervor and excitement. We download a fitness app, join a gym, or start walking with a work-out buddy. We set out faithfully on our endeavor, maybe even making it a month or two, perhaps even seeing some results. However, then we decide to take a week off. Now, I can tell you from personal experience, that anything longer than a day off in an exercise program can be a bad thing. Before long, a couple of days off will turn into a week, and before we know it, we don't have any desire whatsoever to pick back up where we left off. That is why so many people fail when it comes to finishing what they start: whether it be an exercise program or book. We are such an undisciplined society as a whole (and there are exceptions, and I hope you are one of them), that sometimes when we don't "feel" like doing something, we simply don't. And that is why we fail. On the other hand, maybe there is a valid reason why we stop exercising. Maybe two months in to our very successful exercise program, we experience an obstacle: we get the flu. Most people can't exercise when they are losing the contents of their stomachs or running a fever. Hence, taking a break when we're sick is a valid excuse for forgoing an exercise routine. But what happens when the flu passes? Do we resume the routine, or do we give up? It's hard for many people in this position to resume, and consequently, why most people revert to their pre-exercise days. They are physically drained, and exercising does take a certain amount of time out of each day.

This is exactly what happens when writing a book. We take time off, but resuming that habit is difficult, as it takes time and concentration. My advice is this: if you have to take a break, which is acceptable and even required at times, pick a date when you plan to resume. Make it plausible and doable, or you are setting yourself up for failure.

Know this: there are some people out there who are able to start a project, shelve it for a few weeks, months, or even years and then come back to it. It can be done, and I know because I was one of them. I had a case of what is known in writing circles as "writer's block", and you might find yourself facing that from time to time. When you do, if you step back, the longer of a respite you take, the harder it will be to come back to it. So make your break as short as you possibly can; when you resume, work as hard as you can to regain lost ground and get yourself back on track, hopefully this time until the project is completed.

Write anyway. If you don't want to stop writing altogether during unexpected events, another way of dealing with unexpected real-life obstacles is that you can keep writing in the midst of the chaos. It may not be the quality or quantity of writing that you are accustomed to, but it's still something. Schedule thirty minutes a day where you sequester yourself from the pressures or distractions that you are forced to deal with—and write. Even if it isn't your best writing, allowing yourself an opportunity to write and keeping on track will make you feel better and gain more confidence. At this stage, it is best not to be concerned with word count or length. Focus instead on the fact that you are still able to make progress—even in the midst of a busy and stressful time. Recognize and affirm yourself in the midst of the storm.

Remember, during some of the busiest and stressful times of our lives, we still need to find the time to slow down, and taking thirty minutes out of your day to write is not going to hurt you. In fact, it will give you the motivation to return to your mission with more intensity when circumstances and time allow.

In addition to unexpected events, there are times in life when writers lose the will to write and writing becomes a burden. What do you do on those days when you don't feel inspired to write? My advice is this: force yourself to do it anyway, even if it is just for a bit. If you don't learn anything else in this lesson, please learn this. The only way for you to meet your goals is to keep writing. I know it sounds simplified, but it's true. You have to write, even when you're hungry, tired, angry, lost, delirious, and just plain fed up. My point is that you have to write, and write, and write, in all seasons of life. When you do get writer's block, I say, "write anyway." Even if it isn't your best work and you later change the direction you are finding writing is taking, it's better to write something than not to have written at all.

So to recap, it is vital that you set a schedule to attain your goals and stick with it, even when you don't want to. If you want to develop a habit of writing, then discipline is instrumental in making it happen. You can give yourself some flexibility, but the more discipline you require, the stricter your schedule needs to be. If you struggle with discipline, start with the daily schedule. If you are able to meet deadlines, even sometimes in the eleventh hour, and like to write when the inspiration hits, then go with the monthly schedule. If you are somewhere in between, and your busy life activities don't allow you to write daily, follow the weekly schedule.

The second step is creating the mindset of discipline so you can adhere to this schedule. Without it, your schedule will be as meaningless as the paper you print it out on. The important thing is figuring out when to schedule writing time. If you don't do this, you will never get any writing project off the ground, let alone finish it.

To Share or Not to Share: Publishing

As you become more confident in your writing and establish more consistent writing habits, you will have to answer some serious questions. Will there ever come a time when you will feel inclined to share what you have written? If so, in what forum will you do so? What are the ramifications or consequences if you do? How will your friends and family react if you decide to share? How do you know if your writing even classifies as "good enough" or worthy of publishing? Where do you begin?

These are all questions that anyone who makes writing a lifestyle or even a hobby will need to answer. While it is unlikely anyone can make a living off of writing—unless you have extensive training and/or get lucky like some of the famous authors—you can do it for multiple reasons beyond just a monetary reward, fame, or fortune.

In my experiences, there are three common ways that I have found that people find monetary reward in sharing their creative projects: 1) writing for publications or websites; 2) writing a personal blog or ongoing commentary; and 3) writing to publish a more extensive creative work, such as a book or series of shorter works, either through traditional or self publishing. If you add in other creative works that begin as written works but move into other mediums such as podcasts, videos, audio recordings, or music, the opportunities are as infinite as the mind can conceive.

Today, it is simple to get your written work onto the computer screen and phones of friends and strangers alike. Whether it be a rant on a social post, content on a personal website, or a written contribution to another website, the public dissemination of your written work can literally take minutes, if not seconds to reach the masses. This is both a blessing and a curse. On one hand, it's virtually free and quick. On the other hand, it's virtually free and quick. This equates to the simple fact that anyone with a computer and a bit of know-how can share ideas with a few keystrokes and the click of the mouse. This is great news for the aspiring writer. Never has it been easier to publish a book, a podcast, a blog, or other personal means to share your work. It takes very little capital and a bit of education and research, but it can be done. So, if you want to share your work, there is nothing to stop you.

Wrapping Up

Writing permeates everything we do in our lives, especially in this electronic age. There is likely not a day that goes by where you don't use writing to communicate, even informally, in some way with those in your life. As this self-study has hopefully shown you, writing has the chance to be transformative in your life—as well as others. Hopefully, you, like many others, will make writing a lifestyle. If so, don't be afraid to embrace the power that comes with this valuable tool. At the end of the day, the fate of your writing journey—or lack thereof—rests with you. So I encourage you: get in the boat and see where the journey will take you!

Writing for Reflection

1. *Would you describe yourself as a disciplined person? Why/why not?*

2. *What are the obstacles that you foresee could prevent you from writing or achieving your goals?*

3. *When you get overwhelmed with life, how do you typically respond?*

4. *If you get overwhelmed, do you see yourself putting off writing or using it as a means of escape? Explain.*

5. *What is your plan in regard to writing as you wind down this study?*

www.ingramcontent.com/pod-product-compliance
Lightning Source LLC
Chambersburg PA
CBHW040154110726
48005CB00018B/2760